IN THE ZONE

BASKETBALL

Rennay Craats

 WEIGL PUBLISHERS INC.

Published by Weigl Publishers Inc.
350 5th Avenue, Suite 3304, PMB 6G
New York, NY 10118-0069

Website: www.weigl.com

Library of Congress Cataloging-in-Publication Data

Craats, Rennay.
 Basketball / Rennay Craats.
    p. cm. -- (In the Zone)
 Includes index.
 ISBN 978-1-60596-128-6 (hard cover : alk. paper) -- ISBN 978-1-60596-129-3 (soft cover : alk. paper)
 1. Basketball--Juvenile literature. I. Title.
 GV885.1.C73 2010
 796.323--dc22

                          2009005606

Printed in China
1 2 3 4 5 6 7 8 9 13 12 11 10 09

All of the Internet URLs given in the book were valid at the time of publication. However, due to the
dynamic nature of the Internet, some addresses may have changed, or sites may have ceased to exist
since publication. While the author and publisher regret any inconvenience this may cause readers, no
responsibility for any such changes can be accepted by either the author or the publisher.

Every reasonable effort has been made to trace ownership and to obtain permission to reprint
copyright material. The publishers would be pleased to have any errors or omissions brought to their
attention so that they may be corrected in subsequent printings.

Weigl acknowledges Getty Images as its primary image supplier for this title.

Illustrations
Kenzie Browne: pages 9, 10 Left.

Heather C. Hudak Project Coordinator
Terry Paulhus Design
Kenzie Browne Layout

CONTENTS

What is Basketball?

Slam dunks are shots where the player jumps above the net and drives the ball into the basket.

D r. James Naismith taught university physical education in Springfield, Massachusetts. In the winter, his students did not have many games to play inside. He decided to create a new game. He asked a janitor to hang two peach baskets at either end of the gymnasium. Players bounced a soccer ball down the court and tried to throw it into the peach baskets. Within 10 years, metal hoops with nets sewn around the edges replaced the baskets. A **backboard** was added so the ball would not land in the crowd after a shot. Finally, the soccer ball was replaced by a larger, leather ball. Teams in the early 1900s played basketball as we know it today.

■ Dr. Naismith coached many early basketball teams.

Basketball is played by two teams of five. Games often consist of two 20-minute halves. In professional basketball, there are four 12-minute quarters.

To win, a team needs to score more points than its opponent. The offensive team is the one with the ball. Its members **dribble** the ball down the court and try to shoot it into the basket. The defensive team tries to stop them from scoring. Baskets from within the **three-point line** are worth two points. Baskets from outside the three-point line are worth three points.

Sports History

Read about Dr. James Naismith and the beginnings of basketball at www.naismithmuseum.com.

Getting Ready to Play

Basketball players do not need much equipment. The game does not involve contact, so players do not wear padding.

Players wear jerseys with a number on the back. These shirts often do not have sleeves, so players can easily shoot or pass the ball. This style of shirt is also cooler for the players.

Basketball players wear loose-fitting shorts. They are comfortable for the players and allow them to move easily.

The most important piece of equipment for basketball players is shoes. The shoes are light, so players can run quickly. Shoes with rubber bottoms stop players from slipping on the floor. Shoes also have support for the players' ankles to prevent injuries.

Players shoot the ball at the basket. The metal hoop is almost twice as wide as a basketball. The netting hanging from the basket is often made of nylon rope.

The basket is attached to a backboard. The backboard is made of wood, **fiberglass**, or graphite. Backboards keep the ball from going out of bounds every time it is shot. The players bounce the ball off the backboard into the net.

National Basketball Association (NBA) backboards are flat and transparent. A small square is often painted on backboards to help players aim their shots.

Basketballs are made of rubber or leather. The inside of the ball is a rubber bag filled with air. Players can add air to the ball to keep it firm. This gives the ball its bounce.

Basketball is played on a surface called a court. The baskets, which are 10 feet (3 meters) high, hang at either end of the court. The court has many lines and circles painted on it. The boundaries are marked by the baseline and the sideline. Players cannot step outside of these lines with the ball.

The game begins at the center circle. From there, players run up and down the court to score baskets and try to stop the other team from scoring. The lines on the court tell them where they have to shoot from to get three points. The lines also show them where to line up for **free throws**.

Courts in the NBA are usually 94 feet (29 meters) long and 50 feet (15 m) wide.

Sports Tips

To learn how to play better basketball, surf over to www.betterbasketball.com/basketball-court-dimensions.

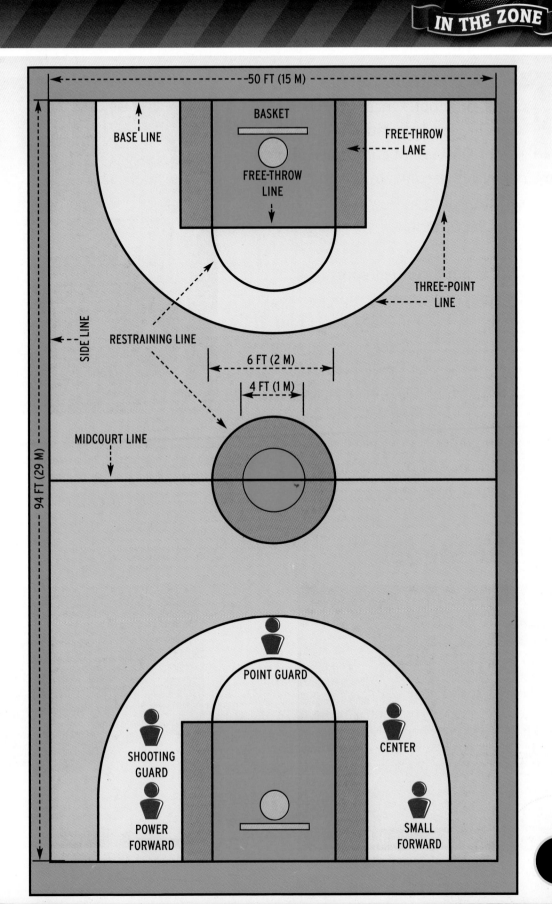

─ 50 FT (15 M) ─

BASE LINE

BASKET

FREE-THROW
LANE

FREE-THROW
LINE

THREE-POINT
LINE

RESTRAINING LINE

SIDE LINE

6 FT (2 M)

4 FT (1 M)

MIDCOURT LINE

94 FT (29 M)

POINT GUARD

SHOOTING
GUARD

CENTER

POWER
FORWARD

SMALL
FORWARD

The player with the ball has to dribble, pass, or shoot. Once the player touches the ball with both hands, he or she cannot continue dribbling. Players have 24 seconds to shoot at the basket. If they do not, they have to give the ball to the other team.

Basketball is not a **contact sport**. If a defensive player pushes, bumps, or knocks another player, he or she is given a **foul**. If the foul occurs as a player is shooting at the basket, he or she is given two free throws. If the shot goes in the basket, the player is given two points for the basket plus one foul shot. Foul shots are worth one point each. The other team cannot block or interfere with these penalty shots.

Players swarm the net after a shot is made to catch a possible missed shot that may bounce off the backboard or basket. They are not allowed to touch the ball if it is above the basket.

Get the Signal

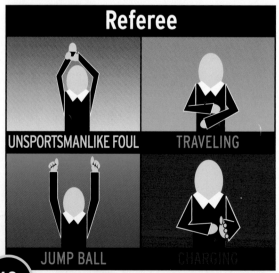

Referee

UNSPORTSMANLIKE FOUL

TRAVELING

JUMP BALL

CHARGING

Coaches help players understand the game and hone their skills.

If the foul occurs at any other time, there is a **throw-in**. The member of the fouled team takes the ball out of bounds and throws it in to his or her teammates. A throw-in also occurs when the ball is thrown or knocked out of bounds. The last team to touch the ball before it bounces out of bounds loses **possession**. The other team throws the ball in. Throw-ins are used after a team scores. The team that was scored upon throws the ball in from the baseline and tries to score at the other end.

Referees can penalize the team for arguing by giving the other team free throws.

The referee and umpire keep order on the court. The referee watches what is happening close to the basket. The umpire watches the other players. If they see players breaking the rules, they blow their whistles to stop the play. The referee makes the final decisions. If players or coaches argue with the referee, they can be thrown out of the game.

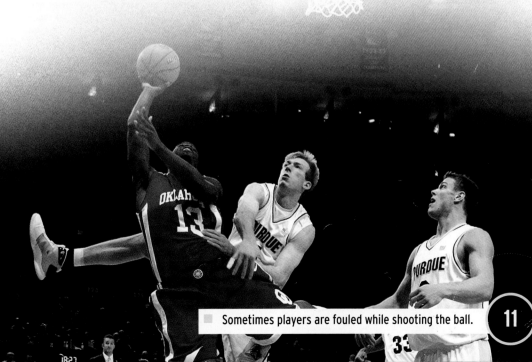

Sometimes players are fouled while shooting the ball.

Positions

There are three positions on a basketball team. The center is the tallest player on the team. Centers take the **jump ball** at the beginning of the game. The centers from each team meet at the center circle. The referee throws the ball straight up in the air. The centers try to tip the ball to their teammates, who are standing outside the circle. Centers also stay close to the basket to catch rebounds, or missed shots. Being tall helps them reach higher and catch the ball.

A jump ball is taken if players from opposing teams touch the ball at the same time before it goes out of bounds. The jump ball is then taken at the nearest circle.

Players must work together to defend the net.

Guards control the plays on the court. They are good dribblers and fast on their feet. Point guards usually bring the ball down the court and pass it to other players. These players can then shoot. Shooting guards are good dribblers and good shooters. They can shoot well from anywhere on the court. It is often the guards who shoot three-point shots.

Forwards stay close to the basket. They usually stand on either side of the basket. Small forwards are good shooters. They make many of the shots at the basket. Power forwards are taller. They help the center rebound and make baskets from the bottom of the court.

A team has possession of the ball when dribbling, passing, or holding the ball.

Forwards have to practice shooting close under the basket.

Sports Stars

To read about the stars behind these positions, visit the Basketball Hall of Fame at www.hoophall.com.

Many children grow up playing basketball at their school yards and playgrounds. They often join community or school teams to learn the skills of the game. College and university basketball teams are great places to get experience and get noticed by the National Basketball Association. Players at the college level want to make the final four.

Like Grant Hill, many college stars make names for themselves in the NBA.

The final four is a college play-off that is watched by millions of people. The play-off is called March Madness. Many players on successful teams in March Madness get **scouted** by professional basketball teams, but not all professional basketball players go to college. Some outstanding players are noticed while they are in junior and senior high.

Cheering on teammates is important at all levels of play.

Sports Teams

Follow your favorite teams at www.nba.com.

Most young basketball players dream of playing in the NBA. Professional basketball players play 82 games each season to make the play-offs. The top eight teams in each division play each other. These are called the Conference Championships. The two winning teams play each other for the NBA Championships. The Boston Celtics have won the championships the most times, with seventeen titles.

Practicing with friends can improve both skill and endurance.

Some players are scouted when they are 17 or 18 years old.

Superstars of the Sport

Basketball has seen many heroes since the NBA was formed in 1949. Many of these players have inspired children to play the game, too.

23 Michael Jordan

POSITION: Guard
TEAM: Chicago Bulls
SIGNED TO THE MAJORS: 1984

CAREER FACTS:

- In the tenth grade, Michael was cut from the varsity basketball team and only made junior varsity.
- Michael led the NBA in scoring nine times and was named Most Valuable Player (MVP) five times.
- Michael led the Bulls to six NBA championships.
- Michael briefly retired from playing basketball in 1993. During the time he was retired, he played professional baseball for one season.
- Many fans, coaches, and critics think Michael was the best player to ever play basketball.

33 Larry Bird

POSITION: Forward
TEAM: Boston Celtics
SIGNED TO THE MAJORS: 1979

CAREER FACTS:

- In Larry's last season, 1991-1992, he earned more than $7 million. The average salary in the league was just more than $1 million!
- Larry was voted Most Valuable Player three times.
- Few of Larry's coaches in college thought he would make the NBA. He worked at basketball all the time and proved them wrong.
- The year before Larry joined the Celtics, the team had won 29 and lost 53 games. With Larry, the team turned their record around, winning 61 and losing only 21 games.
- In 1985-86, Larry finished in the top 10 in five categories, including scoring, steals, and free-throws. It was one of the greatest seasons ever for any player.

13

Wilt Chamberlain

POSITION: Center
TEAM: Los Angeles Lakers
SIGNED TO THE MAJORS: 1959

CAREER FACTS:
- Wilt was a Harlem Globetrotter.
- In 1962, Wilt had the league's highest points per game average. He scored an average of 50.4 points every time he played.
- Wilt's 1962 record for scoring 100 points in a game has never been beaten.

- At 7 feet 1 inch (2.2 m), Wilt was the NBA's first giant superstar.
- Wilt led the league in rebounds 11 times and was the top scorer seven times in a row.

6

Bill Russell

POSITION: Center
TEAM: Boston Celtics
SIGNED TO THE MAJORS: 1956

CAREER FACTS:
- Bill was 6 feet 10 inches (2.1 m) tall.
- In his first year, Bill was the only African American player on the team.
- With Bill as the center, the Celtics won 11 championships in 13 years. Eight of these wins were in a row.

- At 32 years old, Bill became the first African American to coach any major professional sports team. He coached his old team, the Boston Celtics.
- Bill was named the best basketball player ever by the Professional Basketball Writers Association of America in 1980.

Superstars of Today

The basketball stars of today are breaking records and amazing fans.

23 LeBron James

POSITION: Forward
TEAM: Cleveland Cavaliers
SIGNED TO THE MAJORS: 2003

CAREER FACTS:
- LeBron was the 2003-2004 NBA **Rookie** of the Year. He was the first Cavalier and youngest player to win this honor.
- LeBron is the NBA's youngest player to score 1,000 points.
- LeBron played on the U.S. Olympic team in 2004 and 2008.
- LeBron is 6 feet 8 inches (2 m) tall.

13 Steve Nash

POSITION: Point Guard
TEAM: Phoenix Suns
SIGNED TO THE MAJORS: 1996

CAREER FACTS:
- In 2006, *Time* magazine named Nash one of the 100 most influential people in the world.
- Steve won the NBA MVP award in 2005 and 2006.
- In 2007, Nash received the J. Walter Kennedy Citizenship Award, given to players who make outstanding contributions to community work.
- Steve has a sociology degree from Santa Clara University.

24

Kobe Bryant

POSITION: Shooting Guard
TEAM: Los Angeles Lakers
SIGNED TO THE MAJORS: 1996

CAREER FACTS:

- Kobe was voted the NBA's MVP in 2008.
- He was the youngest player to score 20,000 points, beating Wilt Chamberlain's record.
- In the 2004-2005 season, Kobe hit 43 free throws in a row. This broke Gail Goodrich's team record of 40.
- Kobe's parents named him after a Japanese steakhouse in Philadelphia.
- When he was young, Kobe thought he would become a pro-soccer player.

23

Cappie Pondexter

POSITION: Guard
TEAM: Phoenix Mercury
SIGNED TO THE MAJORS: 2006

CAREER FACTS:

- Cappie wears number 23 in honor of Michael Jordan. During her rookie year, Cappie was named to the All-Star game.
- In 2005, Cappie was co-captain of the USA World University Games Team.
- Cappie was named the 2007 WNBA Finals MVP.
- Cappie was a member of Team USA at the Beijing Olympics.

19

Staying Healthy

Basketball is a fast game of running and jumping. To keep up with the rest of the team, basketball players need to stay healthy. A balanced diet of fruit, vegetables, meat, breads, and cereals helps keep their bodies running well. These healthy foods provide important vitamins, minerals, fiber, and proteins that keep players working at their best.

Eating a balanced meal helps keep athletes fit.

Milk is an important part of a healthy diet.

Basketball players need to keep their muscles in shape, too. Stretching is important to prevent injuries. Players should stretch out their shoulders, back, and legs before stepping onto the court. There are also simple ways to strengthen leg muscles. Ski tucks help with strength and jumping.

To train with ski tucks, players stand with their feet together and jump straight in the air. They pull their knees into their chests. Each time they do the drill, they try to jump higher. To further improve their jumping, they stand against a wall and jump up as high as they can. They stretch as far up the wall as possible and try to reach a higher point every day.

It is important to stretch before and after playing a sport.

Basketball teams do special exercise drills to practice their moves.

jr.nba   jr.wnba

Sports Food

To learn more about eating healthy, go to www.mypyramid.gov.

Basketball Brain Teasers

Test your knowledge of this fast-paced sport by trying to answer these basketball brain teasers!

Q What is the purpose of the backboard?

A Backboards keep the ball from going out of bounds every time it is shot. The players bounce the ball off the backboard into the net.

Q How long is a basketball game?

A Games often consist of two 20-minute halves. In professional basketball, there are four 12-minute quarters.

Q What are the roles of the referee and the umpire?

A The referee and umpire keep order on the court. The referee watches what is happening close to the basket. The umpire watches the other players.

A LeBron James was the youngest player to win NBA Rookie of the Year.

Q Who was the youngest player to win NBA Rookie of the Year?

A There are three positions on a basketball team.

Q How many positions are there on a basketball team?

A Professional basketball players play 82 games each season to make the play-offs.

Q How many games must professional players play before making the play-offs?

Glossary

backboard: the rectangular board to which the basket is attached

contact sport: a sport where physical contact between players, such as tackling and checking, is allowed

dribble: bounce the ball off the floor with one hand at a time

fiberglass: a material made of very fine strands of glass

foul: a penalty for illegal contact

free throws: shots that a fouled player takes from the foul line—no one can try to block this shot

jump ball: when the referee tosses the ball straight up between two opposing players, and the players try to knock the ball to their teammates

possession: control of the ball by a player or team

rookie: a player in his or her first year

scouted: being noticed by representatives of stronger sports teams

three-point line: the large half-circle drawn toward the outside of the basket

throw-in: putting the ball back in play from out of bounds

Index